T0113853

The
Melodies
of Christ

RONALD WILLIAM CADMUS

WESTBOW
PRESS®
A DIVISION OF THOMAS NELSON
& ZONDERVAN

WestBow Press books may be ordered through booksellers or by contacting:

WestBow Press
A Division of Thomas Nelson & Zondervan
1663 Liberty Drive
Bloomington, IN 47403
www.westbowpress.com
844-714-3454

Because of the dynamic nature of the Internet, any web addresses or links contained in this book may have changed since publication and may no longer be valid. The views expressed in this work are solely those of the author and do not necessarily reflect the views of the publisher, and the publisher hereby disclaims any responsibility for them.

Any people depicted in stock imagery provided by Getty Images are models, and such images are being used for illustrative purposes only.
Certain stock imagery © Getty Images.

Scripture quotations are from the New Revised Standard Version Bible, copyright © 1989 the Division of Christian Education of the National Council of the Churches of Christ in the United States of America. Used by permission. All rights reserved.

ISBN: 978-1-6642-7024-4 (sc)
ISBN: 978-1-6642-7028-2 (hc)
ISBN: 978-1-6642-7025-1 (e)

Library of Congress Control Number: 2022911581

Print information available on the last page.

WestBow Press rev. date: 05/30/2023

This book is dedicated:

to the music directors, educators, choral groups, church and college choirs, and other inspiring voices who fill my soul with deep faith, praise, and honor to God.

to Larry Parsons, choir director at West Virginia Wesleyan College's chorale, chapel, and tour choir, whose music helped me to choose something like a star to stay my life upon and be stayed. His life fills my heart with song.

to Ruth Liable, organist and choir director at the Evangelical United Brethren Church in Newark, New Jersey, where I was baptized as an infant, confirmed as a thirteen year old, and where—each Sunday at her invitation—I sat next to her on the organ bench, mesmerized by her triumphant postludes. When I was in seminary, Ruth died, leaving me her library of church anthems.

to my parents, Henry and Bertha Cadmus, who filled my life and our home with the melodies of Christ, singing of God's perfect love and helping my young footsteps walk where Jesus walked.

to Irene Stoller and Helene Klein, Mom's sisters, who together the three of them shaped our lives with their glorious voices. They taught me that "if with all our hearts we truly seek Him, we will surely find Him." Their heavenly voices fill my heart today.

to Valerie Klein Whyte, Althea Klein, and Courtney Whyte May, who continue the tradition, blending voices and strings in the melodies of Christ.

to those who have opened their hearts to my words by setting my text to their inspiring music.

"Ron Cadmus uses words in the same way a composer uses notes to convey his message. He carefully selects each word to ensure it will touch the soul in a new and meaningful way. His verse is never trite, never sappy but always simple, elegant, and moving. It will give you pause to think about the amazing grace and love of God. It will draw you closer to the Divine. *The Melodies of Christ* will give you a new perspective on who our wonderful Savior is and how His life can be intertwined in ours. To live an abundant life on this earth is to live a life dedicated to Christ.

"I have set several of these poems to music, and each time I am amazed at how easily the notes fall on to the page. The great artist Michelangelo believed that the sculptures were already in the stones and simply needed someone to bring them out; I have found that to be true with Ron's words as well. The melodies exist in the words on the page, and all they need is a willing person to bring them out. As you read this collection of poems, may the melodies in your heart begin to sing and your spirit begin to soar. Let the words of these pages penetrate your heart and soul; they will truly bring you comfort and joy."

—R. Kevin Boesiger, composer, director of blended music and kingdom growth at Covenant Presbyterian Church in Omaha, Nebraska

"One day, about ten years ago, I received an email from a Reverend Ronald W. Cadmus that indicated he'd heard some of my music and, being a writer and lyricist, was interested in collaborating with me. My first reaction was, *Oh boy! Not another 'you have to hear my son play the violin' moment.* That was until he sent me the lyrics for "God's Whisper," a beautiful and profound statement on the power and beauty of faith—a theme that permeates almost all his writings—and a lyric I immediately wanted to set to music. Thus began an over decade long collaboration, one that has produced over a dozen pieces for chorus, many of which have been published and entered the standard repertoire of choirs around the world.

"Working with Ron has been a joy. He is a writer with the extraordinary ability to express his convictions about God, faith, art, and the beauty of nature in a way that captures its intrinsic universality without resorting to heavy-handiness or preachiness. He knows and relishes the value of collaboration and is always willing to keep an open mind. I am blessed to have found both a dear friend and creative partner and learned that you never know when your neighbor's son might turn out to be Joshua Bell."

—Robert. S. Cohen, international composer

Contents

The Melodies of Christ

Foreword

I've always been mesmerized by poetry. In fact, it's probably safe to say I've loved it since my childhood. I still remember the quizzical look my parents gave me when, at a very young age, I asked for a volume of poetry for Christmas.

What is it about poetry that makes it so compelling? I'm not sure I know the answer. A fine poem has the power to stir the imagination and to enlarge the mind. It can help us see ourselves—and others—in a new and fresh light. In short, poetry has the ability to *transform* us.

As people striving to grow in our relationships with Christ, we undoubtedly benefit when we spend time reading poetry that is devotional in nature. Devotional poetry specifically hones in on the work and persons of the triune God, as well as various aspects of the Christian life, like conviction, confession, forgiveness, self-sacrifice, worship, and love. And, of course, good devotional poetry feeds us spiritually. It causes us to grow in holiness, and it turns our hearts and minds toward the things of heaven.

The volume you're holding in your hands contains some of the finest devotional poetry around, as well as generous amounts of beautifully crafted song lyrics and texts. In the following pages, Ron Cadmus will help you grow in your knowledge of God's grace, mercy, and incomparable love. Ron writes with the heart of a pastor, the inquisitiveness of a scholar, and the creativity of an artist, and he brings astonishing insights and honesty to each line of prose.

Read this book slowly. In fact, take time to savor it. Reading sacred poetry and lyrics should not feel like a race to the finish line. As you read, open your heart to what God might want to teach you. If you do so, Ron's words can become a vehicle used by the Holy Spirit to bring you into a deeper, more fulfilling relationship with Him. Of course, outside of private worship, this book can also be effectively used as a resource for public worship. You'll find ample material here that can easily be incorporated into responsive readings and liturgies.

As a composer, I've had the opportunity to collaborate with Ron in the world of choral music. His heart for the Lord is obvious, as is his desire to share the light of Christ with a darkened world. I'm privileged to count him as a friend, and I'm honored to provide this foreword for his latest manuscript.

By the way, I still have that first volume of poetry my parents bought for me when I was a youngster. It's sitting on the bookshelf beside my desk along with the works of other writers I've discovered through the years. And, to my collection of such luminaries as Rossetti, Donne, and Milton, I'm proud to add this new volume by Cadmus. Spend some time with this one. You'll be glad you did.

Brad Nix, composer, arranger, orchestrator, editor, the Lorenz Corporation

The Melodies of Christ

Preface

The whole life of Christ was a continual Passion; others die
martyrs but Christ was born a martyr. He found a Golgotha even
in Bethlehem, where he was born; for to his tenderness then the
straws were almost as sharp as the thorns after, and the manger
as uneasy at first as his cross at last. His birth and his death were
but one continual act, and his Christmas Day and his Good Friday
are but the evening and morning of one and the same day. And
as even his birth is his death, so every action and passage that
manifests Christ to us is his birth, for Epiphany is manifestation.
—John Donne (1572–1631)

My song of love unknown, my Savior's love to me,
love to the loveless shown that they might lovely be.
O who am I that for my sake my Lord
should take frail flesh, and die?

He came from heaven's throne salvation to bestow;
the world that was his own would not its Savior know.
But O my Friend, my Friend indeed, who
at my need his life did spend!

Sometimes we strew his way, and his sweet praises sing,
resounding all the day hosannas to our King.
Then "Crucify!" is all our breath, and for his death we thirst and cry.

Unheeding, we will have our dear Lord made away,
a murderer to save, the prince of life to slay.
Yet steadfast he to suffering goes, that he
his foes from thence might free.

Here might I stay and sing, no story so divine:
never was love, dear King, never was grief like thine.
This is my Friend, in whose sweet praise I
all my days could gladly spend.
—Samuel Crossman (1664)

The illuminating thoughts by John Donne and the compelling words of Crossman speak to me of the wonderful words of life, of *The Melodies of Christ*, and the song of life that His life conveys. The prose, poems, and lyrics in this book are the melodies of Christ's praise within my heart. We hear many discussions today about the traditional hymns and anthems being in conflict with the contemporary songs that now fill our sanctuaries to the point we designate two separate worship services on Sunday mornings. This book reveals how the traditional and the contemporary are blended in our forms of praise and adoration and the meaning and beauty each brings to our worship of God.

In *The Melodies of Christ* we have a rich wealth of the manifestations of Christ in words that create an epiphany of understanding in more intimate ways, which allows us to proclaim the song within our soul and the song of love in our hearts for Christ. I pray that my words might inspire new epiphanies in worship, liturgy, seasonal celebrations, and in your prayerful contemplative moments as you journey in faith. Adapt the readings by turning some of them into responsive readings, and use others as dramatic readings during Advent and Lent. Let their melodies magnify the sacrifice of Christ in your Maundy Thursday, Tenebrae, and Good Friday reflections. As you spend time with this book, hear the music and the melodies. Mary offered her Magnificat to God. Angels sang in the skies over Bethlehem. The crowds sang Hosanna waving their Palm Branches. When the disciples left Gethsemane to face Golgotha, they sang a hymn. On Good Friday their melodies turned to wailing, in the requiem of their grief. On Easter the angels proclaimed Alleluia, He is risen.

Here might I stay and sing, no story so divine:
never was love, dear King, never was grief like thine.
This is my Friend, in whose sweet praise I
all my days could gladly spend.
—Samuel Crossman (1664)

May your lives be filled with *The Melodies of Christ*. Sing them over again and again and again! Gladly spend your time with the melodies of Christ's love.

Ronald W. Cadmus

I waited patiently for the L<small>ORD</small>;
he inclined to me and heard my cry.
He drew me up from the desolate pit,
out of the miry bog,
and set my feet upon a rock,
making my steps secure.
He put a new song in my mouth,
a song of praise to our God.
—Psalm 40:1–3 (NRSV)

Let the word of Christ dwell in you richly; teach and
admonish one another in all wisdom; and with gratitude in
your hearts sing psalms, hymns, and spiritual songs to God.
—Colossians 3:16 (NRSV)

Rejoice in the Lord, O you righteous.
Praise befits the upright.
Praise the Lord with the lyre;
make melody to him with the harp of ten strings.
Sing to him a new song;
play skillfully on the strings, with loud shouts.
—Psalm 33:1–3 (NRSV)

It was not only Peter who said, "Even if I have to die
with you, I will not deny you." They all said these same
words. They then sang a hymn and left the upper room.
—Matthew 25:35

The Melodies of Christ
Prayer

To Love As God Loves—
A Prayerful Melody

To love as God loves,
To give as God gives,
To care as God cares,
To be wings that lift,
To be tender with a touch,
To forgive as Christ has forgiven me,
To be His alone,
To see as God sees.
To be held in God's embrace
To hold Him in my soul's arms.
To look into His face—
So full of knowing,
His compassion showing
In every word,
His grace bestowing
On those who long for love,
On those who dream of peace.
On those He calls His own
His mercies never cease.
Let my voice sing as God sings.
Let my heart
Love as God loves.
May my life be a melody of
gratitude
and unending praise.
Amen.

The Gift of Advent Waiting

The light draws near.
The world is waiting
In darkness, fear, and hope
For One who brings streams of
mercy and redeeming grace.
A star moves slowly in celestial space—
Through its radiant beams God's love on earth bestowing.
We see God in a baby's face,
In a halo's glow,
In a sacred night.
We hear God's voice in a baby's cry;
Peace and joy from heaven draws nigh—
The gift of Advent waiting.

The light draws near in Advent waiting,
The King of Glory, gentle lamb.
For Christ our Lord, the wondrous gift of our salvation.
A Savior's birth, so long expected,
In humble manger lies.
God is with us,
The joy of all creation,
While we wait …
Waiting for
A light of joy,
A light of peace,
A light of truth,
A light of faith,
A light of hope,
A light of love

A light of life—
The light of Christ eternal.
Mary's little Child,
The gift of Advent waiting.

In the Manger of Love's Appearing

From heaven to earth, the love of Christ is nearing.
God gives the precious gift of Christmas,
A crown of righteousness,
To those who love Christ's appearing.

He brings peace to treasure,
Pure joy beyond measure,
And the promise of salvation.
Stars show their adoration,
Their bright hope shining
On love that slumbers,
On love that slumbers
In the manger of His appearing.

From heaven to earth, the love of Christ is nearing.
God gives the precious gift of Christmas,
A crown of righteousness,
To those who love Christ's appearing.

Hosts of angels fill the sky,
Their glad tidings telling,
God has made His dwelling
On earth with every nation.
"Gloria," sings all creation.
God's heart of love, with love our hearts endearing
As a baby slumbers,
As a baby slumbers
In the manger of love's appearing.

So sing of joy at Christmastide;
The star of Christ is nearing.
And wear the crown of righteousness, for loving Christ's appearing.

The Gift of Doves

Mary and Joseph gave God a gift of doves
    To share their joy and deepest love,
A gift so pure of precious doves
    As worthy as their perfect love,
To thank Him for their holy child
    Born on Christmas so meek and mild.

They knew their Lamb was born the whole world to save,
    To one day rise from the grave,
A gift revealing grace and love,
    Salvation born on wings of doves.
God's Word descended from above
    To tell their Son He's God's beloved!

The angels filled the skies with their songs that night
    As peace shone from a star so bright.
Their glorious praise, God's sheer delight,
    His gift of hope our heart's true light.
Lift your hands; give gifts of doves.
    This Christmastide give Christ your love.

Mysterious Night

Mysterious night,
Dark, yet ever bright.
Miracle and love meet in a stable.
Sheep and cattle sleeping.
Angels in the sky.
Alleluia!
Proclaim Christ's birth.

Sweet, gentle, child
Born so meek and mild.
Love of God upon Your face is shining.
Born to be our Savior
With the world we sing,
"Alleluia!
Christ is our King!"

Shepherds and wise men
Following the star
Stand before the hope of their hearts' yearnings,
Searching for the promise—
God's own precious Son.
Alleluia!
Their wand'rings done.

In Bethlehem
God's epiphany
Brings us the glad tidings of salvation,
Fullness of creation.
Loving God, we see—
Alleluia—
Eternity!

Emmanuel,
God with us to dwell,
Bringing joy on earth in Christmas glory.
Everlasting Father,
Prince of Peace, He reigns.
Alleluia!
His love we claim.

In broken bread,
Through the blood He shed,
Miracle and love meet at His table.
Love born in a stable.
Sin nailed on a tree.
Alleluia! Glory to Thee!

The Master's Crib

On this silent Christmas night,
stars fill the skies with dazzling light
to impart the joy God wants us to know,
how love was born, His full grace to show.

Who is this King who gives us life,
redeeming us and all creation through His Holy birth?
Do you know this Jesus child who brings hope and peace
on earth?
Even the ox knows its owner,
The donkey, its master's crib.
Little lambs know their shepherd's voice,
and doves, in pure white innocence,
with the angels spread their wings
to sing their carols and rejoice!

Christ was born in a dusty stable to claim us as His own;
from the newborn baby's cries, a deeper truth was shown.
The love born on a manger bed, would in the distant years
be the blood upon the cross; salvation's love our Lord would
shed,
flowing from a cup on dusty table, mingled with His grieving
tears.

A humble servant, no royal throne, to heal our lives, our sins
atone
through grace bent in a crown of thorns, one day, this child,
to adorn
the precious Savior's head.

Who is this King who gives us life,
to whom wise men bring gifts of gold, their frankincense,
and myrrh?
Do you know this Jesus child, born in us, our second birth?
Even the ox knows its owner,
the donkey, its master's crib
Little lambs know their shepherd's voice,
and doves, in pure white innocence,
with the angels spread their wings
to sing their carols and rejoice!

Let us join these friendly beasts
to sing this blessed holy eve
of love that saved the lost and least.
Let the eastern star above
lead us to Bethlehem's glorious sight
to find the miracle of love,
a babe who knows His cradle is the Master's crib,
where love shines ever bright.

> Even the Ox knows its owner and the donkey his master's crib.
> —Isaiah 1–3 (NRSV)

This Christmas Night

This Christmas night, stars shinning bright
O'er all the earth tell of Christ's birth,
God's love, our hearts with hope illuminating.

On angel wings, the Child God brings
From heav'n to dwell on earth, our King,
To save us from our sin, Emmanuel.

Joy over Bethlehem!
From the East come regal wise men.
Shepherds in wintry fields
Leave their sheep; their fears they yield
And run with haste, on star-lit hills,
Their lonely lives glad tidings fill.

Within the manger stall,
The kings and strangers bow in awe.
Mary, so pure and mild,
Swaddles her holy Child,
while His face shines with the splendor
Of love and grace.

This Christmas night (Gloria),
Stars shining bright (Gloria)
O'er all the earth (in Excelsis)
Tell of Christ's birth (in Excelsis),
God's love our hearts with hope illuminating!
He shall be called
Wonderful, Counselor, Almighty God,

Everlasting Father (in Excelsis),
The Prince of Peace.
This Christmas night,
Stars shining bright
O'er all the earth with
Peace, peace, peace, peace.
(Isaiah 9:6 NRSV)

Lullaby

Lullaby, my sweet baby, close your eyes.
Don't you cry, precious little one.
As the stars touch the darkness of the night,
You, my child, are my heart's bright light.
In my arms I'll hold you close, swaddled in my dreams.
Here you'll find something of love in my arms,
Something of God.
Lullaby, little lambs to watch You sleep;
Life of mine, may Your dreams be sweet.

Soon enough You'll feel the pain this harsh world can bring.
Soon enough Your heart will break, but for now, hear angels
sing.
Lullaby, while the angels watch You sleep.
Life of mine, may Your dreams be sweet.
Lullaby,
Lullaby,
Lullaby,
Here, You're safe with me.
You're safe with me.

Remembering Rachel—A Trinity of Remembrance

What Can Separate Us?

What can separate us?
Nothing!
From God's love?
Nothing!
Height
nor depth
nor walls
can sever love!
In His hands we are securely held.
On His palms our names are written.
In His heart is love's invitation.
In His mind the lost memorized.
In His mercy no life is marginalized.
From His words kindness is spoken.
Through His touch comfort is promised.
In His eyes we are known.
Safe welcoming arms offer asylum;
no greater love was ever shown.
In His presence compassion cheers us
to dry our tears, dispel our fears.
His unfailing love, our consolation,
In His footsteps the path unending
Leads over thresholds, to new life.

Lamentation of Tears

Remember Rachel, who in her weeping
mourned the faces of children who were no more.
Grace is the home
found in the wilderness
that gathers and shelters the innocent
with God's tender,
inseparable love.
God embraces the world's children
evermore.
Nothing!
Nothing
can divide or tear us
from God's love.
Remember,
Remember.
Nothing!
Nothing!!
Remember Rachel.
Remember the children.

Remember the Blessing

God hears the voice of every child.
Where that child is, God is there
to hold each one with His hand.
With chords of kindness,
bonds of love,
God lifts the infant to His cheek.
Bending down to each longing glance,
blessings abound for those who seek.

No loving father would give a stone
to a hungry child who asks for bread.
No loving father would give a stone
to one searching for refuge
or a home.
In God's heart every name is known.
He holds us close; we are His own.
Remember!
Remember
that where you are,
God is there.
In every moment, of joy or fear,
remember
the voice of every child God hears
and brings His peace and blessing
ever near, ever near.
Remember the promised blessing,
God is with us—always here.

(Matthew 7:9 No father would give a stone to a hungry child who asks for bread
Matthew 2: 18 Remember Rachael who in her weeping mourned the children
who would be no more
Hosea 11:4 I led them with cords of human kindness, with ties of love. To
them I was like one who lifts a little child to the cheek, and I bent down to
feed them. New Living Translation NRSV New Revised Standard Version,
Hendrickson Publishers Inc. copyright 1989 by the Division of Christian
Education of the National Council of the Churches of Christ in the USA.)

With Child

She was with child,
Mary, so mild,
chosen to carry
the Hope of the world.
Mary, so mild,
and her little child
born to one day carry earth's every child.

Hunger is with every child -
starving for some bread.
Homeless shelters are with every child -
longing for warm beds.
War is with every child -
crying for a world of peace.
Darkness is with every child -
longing for their fears to cease.

Some homes hold a battered child
who never hears of love.
Some eyes reveal a shattered child
whose dreams cannot fly
to starry skies on wings of doves.

So, Mary mild,
On this holy night, with child,
let your light shine upon and cradle
the children of the earth,
in the manger of God's love,
there to find
the wondrous sign
of peace and joy
through our Savior's birth.
And may His star lead us far
to share our love with every child on earth.

God Who Lights the Christmas Sky

God who lights the Christmas sky, who in peace with us abides.
Star of wonder, lead us home.
Lamb to mother, child to mother,
Fill us with love this Christmastide.

God who lights the Christmas sky, who in joy with us abides.
Star of wonder, lead us home
To the manger to adore Thee.
Fill us with hope this Christmastide.

God who lights the Christmas sky, who in song with us abides.
Star of wonder, lead us home.
Host of angels, sing their glory.
Fill us with praise this Christmastide.

God who lights the Christmas sky, who on straw with us abides.
Star of wonder, lead us home
Where shepherds kneel by starlit hay.
Fill us with thanks this Christmastide.

God who lights the Christmas sky, who in truth with us abides.
Star of wonder, lead us home.
With the wise men, humbly bowing,
Fill us with awe this Christmastide.

God who lights the Christmas sky, who in grace with us abides.
Star of wonder, lead us home
To the child born to save us.
Fill us with life this Christmastide.

God who lights the Christmas sky, who in Christ with us abides.
Star of wonder, lead us home.
Holy Child, meek and mild,
Fill us with light this Christmastide.

Christmas Bells Ringing

I

Christmas bells ringing, the whole world is singing.
The angels are winging; glad tidings they're bringing.
God's love to earth! The Savior's birth!
Gloria in Excelsis!
Christmas bells pealing, bright starlight revealing
Salvation and healing as shepherds are kneeling.
In a small stable in Bethlehem, Christ is born today!
Wonderful counselor, Prince of Peace,
From all our fears and sins release.
Emmanuel,
Joy with us dwells!
Come, all ye faithful, hearts ever grateful.
Christmas bells ringing, the whole world is singing.
The angels are winging; glad tidings they're bringing
God's love to earth! The Savior's birth!
Gloria in Excelsis!
In Excelsis Gloria, Gloria!
Christmas bells are ringing.
Chime their carols,
All the world heralding
Christ the newborn King!
Ding dong, ding dong!
Christmas bells are ringing!
Christ is born today!

II

Tenderly,
Tenderly
The holy mother sings.
Silently,
Silently
The bells of Christmas ring.

Peace on earth,
Peace on earth
Fills all the world tonight.
Ring the bells,
Ring the bells
With joyous sounds so bright.

Come, behold.
Come, behold.
Adore the Child King.
Love is born.
Love is born.
The bells of Christmas ring.

Ring the bells.
Ring the bells.
Hear their music swell.
Ring the bells.
Ring the bells.
God comes to earth to dwell.

Christmas bells,
Christmas bells,
Christmas bells are pealing.
Christ is born,
Christ is born,
God's full love revealing.

III

Hear the bells merrily calling to the manger our glad hearts.
Still, the night, while snowflakes falling.
Peace on earth, God doth impart.

Star of wonder, brightly beaming, shines
o'er Bethlehem this night.
From our sin love's grace redeeming,
Turning darkness into light.

Hear the bells; the sheep are bleating.
See the Lamb of God asleep.
Wise men bring their gifts and greeting.
Friendly beasts their vigil keep.

Hear the bells and angels singing,
spreading joy and hope on earth.
In our hearts salvation bringing.
Let the bells proclaim Christ's birth.

Beneath a Silver Star

Tonight in dreamless sleep,
While silent stars shine brightly
Our hearts welcome a Child—
God's love, purest light.
Born this holy night
Beneath a silver star, in a manger
Where love whispers peace,
Where love whispers joy
For God's little boy.

The stars, o'er Bethlehem
Bring miracles and wonder
From God in heaven yonder.
No star is so bright,
No star is more fair
Than Jesus who slumbers in a stable
Where love whispers peace
Where love whispers joy
For God's little boy.

Stars in their dazzling splendor
Help us to believe.
Just as they glow above,
We were born to share our love.
Let Christ's light shine within you,
And on this Christmas Eve,
Let all who come to the manger
Follow the star and believe, and believe, and believe,
and believe that—

Tonight, in dreamless sleep,
While silent stars shine brightly
Our hearts welcome a Child.
God's love, purest light
Born this holy night
Beneath a silver star, in a manger,
Where love whispers peace, where love whispers joy, for
God's little boy.

Love's Warmest Glow

Still, still, still softly glowing,
Love is born within the light
This silent night.
A miracle stirs in a manger
Bestowing joy
As warm starlight
Whispers of love
On a bed of straw.
Love sings within us,
Illuminating every heart with peace.
All is calm.
All is silent.
All is sacred.
Winter brings its hopeful moment.
The world is changed because of love.
Warmly glowing o'er the earth from heaven above.
See it.
Feel it.
Embrace it.
Trust it.
Believe it.
Hold it in your arms,
This promise born this holy night.
To touch your dreams and longings
Leave every fear with
Winter's shadows.
The heart of Christmas knows
That in its peace is our wholeness

As a miracle swaddles us
With love's warmest glow.
Be still in awe and wonder,
And when the season passes
And we find ourselves again
In the tears of fearful moments
Promised just by living,
Remember, love is never through with us.
Just be still and feel the radiant mystery
Of Christmas, love's warmest glow.
Promised just by loving.

The Songs of Candles

Oh, candle, in sacred space,
Tiny flame reaching high
Upon holy altars
Like towering columns of cathedral naves,
Disperse your light the distance to
Our waiting hearts.
God's whisper is
The breath the wick
Needs to lighten
The world with love.
Swaying,
Illuminating,
Warm,
Quiet,
Flickering,
Still,
Radiant,
Calming,
Peaceful,
Tranquil.
Penetrating space,
The earth,
Our hearts,
Minds,
Eyes
With their radiant peace and promise,
Casting their soft, gentle
Grace

Upon
The shadows
Of our living
To show the way.
Love calls us
To be light,
To be love that glows
In days of deepening darkness,
In moments of harsh grief and pain
When all seems lost.
When joy can't find its voice
Be still and hear,
Be still and hear
The gleaming
Songs of candles.

John the Baptist

A voice set apart,
A wilderness cry
Boldly confessing.
I am the voice
Shouting.
"Prepare a way in your heart,
For He who will come
Bringing truth,
Giving life,
Revealing God's kingdom,
The Way of Salvation,
Forgiving our sins,
Healing all strife."

Step into the waters.
Let your deep thirst
And yearning
Find hope in the stream
With joy overflowing.
Baptized and chosen
We are for a purpose
Hearing our calling
To live as Christ lives;
To embrace one another,
His love always sharing.
The least will be greater
When sins are confessed
When we are washed in His kindness,
In the Spirit we're blessed.

Not a prophet
Nor Elijah
Did John claim to be—
Just a voice set apart
Declaring God's kingdom
Would from sin set us free.
Those who heard John
By his truth were compelled
To kneel in the water
And prepare for the day
When the Messiah
Would come to the Jordan,
And there through John's hand
And the dove that descended
Begin His mission of Salvation's plan.

A voice set apart,
A wilderness cry,
Camel hair for clothing
Ordinary, yet bold,
Preparing a straight way,
For a new life this day.
You are chosen!
With a purpose
To be a life set apart
To share Christ's love from your heart.

(Mark 1: 3 (NRSV) reference "I am a voice crying in the wilderness, prepare ye the way of the Lord, make straight a highway for our God." NRSV New Revised Standard Version, Hendrickson Publishers Inc. copyright 1989 by the Division of Christian Education of the National Council of the Churches of Christ in the USA).

We Worship and Adore You Lord

We worship and adore You, Lord,
With hearts in grateful song
In creed and prayer
Through love we share
In sacrament that heals all wrong.
We thank You for Your love.
We thank You for Your love.

The world displays Your majesty,
All things Your hands create.
The earth, the seas,
The skies, the trees
In harmony they celebrate
The beauty of Your love,
The beauty of Your love.

Behind the dark and dim unknown
You stand with truth and light.
Where virtue fails
And hate is strong
Your Word can give our blindness sight.
The power of Your love,
The power of Your love.

Our prayers lift up our deepest needs
For you to hear our pleas.
Look in our lives
And search our souls;
Help us to change, from sin, set free,

The mercy of Your love,
The mercy of Your love.

The cross and Your unfailing love
Heals all earth's bitter strife.
It is our hope.
It holds us safe
Till we receive eternal life,
The promise of Your love,
The promise of Your love.

In mystery and miracle
Love came to earth to dwell,
To give us strength
And tongues of fire.
Your joy proclaims good news to tell—
The wonders of Your love,
The wonders of Your love.

You call us, Lord, to follow you
In trust and faithfulness.
Let actions, Lord,
Speak beyond words.
Through sharing grace, let us confess
The challenge of Your love,
The challenge of Your love.

Come to Me, Lord

Come to me, Lord.
Come now.
Oh, Savior, hear the secret thoughts within my heart,
and give my
wand'ring spirit rest,
my sin release.
Oh,
come to me, Lord,
kind Lord,
and let Your healing touch embrace the anguish of my soul
With joy, pure light, and words of hope that
take away my fears,
wipe away all tears,
lift the guilt of years.
Through Your grace, Lord,
In this place, Lord,
Let me know the promise to be whole.
I come to You, Lord,
I come.
Now love away my shame
that I have held so long
instead of holding Thee.
My Savior, Jesus,
set my spirit free.
My unfailing friend,
let me faithful be.
Let Your love, Lord,
lead me to peace.

Let Us in the Lord Rejoice

Let us in the Lord rejoice,
Lifting hands and hearts and voice
For His steadfast love and grace.
Let the Lord our God be praised
With our thanks forever raised.

Those who look to God above
Will be filled with all His love
Source of faithfulness and strength,
May we find truth in Your Word,
Seeking justice undeterred.

When we share the holy feast
Yet withhold grace from the cup,
Turn our blindness toward the least,
Heal our schisms as we sup.
God, through mercy, lift us up.

With resolve to do what's right
We bear witness to Your light.
Unconstrained forgiveness share,
Unafraid to seek the lost,
To love and not count the cost.

Through the witness we proclaim,
May it honor Jesus's name.
Sharing Christ, the Word of Life,
Spreading hope that sets all free
To live in eternity.

As we seek to follow You
Let the cross our will renew.
Christ's love to exemplify
Walking humbly by Your side,
In Your Spirit to abide.

Praise the Lord for His Faithfulness

Here in God's presence we gather.
Psalms of hope and praises we bring.
As the waves of the ocean rise
Joyous anthems on wings touch the skies.
Hymns lift our thankful hearts to You.
Of Your majesty we sing.

> Praise the Lord for His faithfulness.
> His music has made our hearts glad.
> With melodies resounding, our love and song abounds.
> In harmonies astounding, God's love shines all around.

Through worship and celebration
As we share the word of life.
Jesus Christ with our tongues we confess.
With our voice our Creator we bless.
Trumpets and pipe raise their offering.
"Blessings flow from Him," we sing.

> Praise the Lord for His faithfulness.
> His music has made our hearts glad.
> With melodies resounding, our love and song abounds.
> In harmonies astounding, God's love shines all around.

> (interlude)

> Praise the Lord for His faithfulness
> His music has made our hearts glad
> With melodies resounding, our love and song abounds
> In harmonies astounding, God's love shines all around.

Almighty and Eternal God, Your Spirit Gives Us Life

Almighty and eternal God, Your spirit gives us life.
We thank You for Your gracious love that heals our sin and
strife.

We magnify the love of God in all we do and say.
He knows our need before we ask and hears us when we pray.

Abundant blessings come from You, the treasure of Your
Word.
You hold us in Your tender heart, with love so undeserved.

When discord tears the church apart, malignant thoughts
destroy.
Turn our strictness from hearts of stone to hearts of flesh
and joy

Lord, let Your peace bring to our world, a hope for humankind
Where harmony must first take birth, within our heart and
mind.

Thanks to God, Awesome in Wonder

Thanks to God, awesome in wonder
For His mighty holiness.
Giver of life, with gifts of splendor,
Love that endures and love to bless.

Take the cup that His hand offers.
Grace to share in holy bread,
The gifts of God, for those who hunger
Their deepest longings will be fed.

Food from the earth, wine to gladden,
Oil to make the face to shine,
Bread to strengthen every weary heart—
The soul at peace, on Christ reclines.

One true God, whose love defends us,
You give life abundantly.
In faithful worship, faithful living
We give You our lives joyfully.

(Psalm 104: 14–15 "food from the earth, wine to gladden, oil to make the
face to shine." English
Standard Version 2016 NRSV New Revised Standard Version, Hendrickson
Publishers Inc. copyright 1989 by the Division of Christian Education of the
National Council of the Churches of Christ in the USA).

Here in the Silence

Here in the silence,
Lord, speak to my yearning,
My heart ever turning
To You for Your love.
       Show me Your face, Lord.
       Help me today, Lord,
       To know the joy of Your grace.
Here in the silence
When fearful shadows
And darkness surround me
Make me always trust Thee
with all my heart and soul.

Your hand will hold me,
Your Spirit enfold me.
My sins forgiving,
When from the depths I cry.

I love You, Lord—my strength
My future, and my rock.
When I am hungry, when I am lost
On wild seas, my life is tossed.
No matter where I wander,
Your faithful love is near.

Here in the silence
I wait for the morning,
True light ever dawning
with Your sweet voice of love.

Here in the silence
I wait for morning,
Wait for the morning.
Here in the silence,
Here in the silence.

God's Whisper

Whoever loves
Finds safety on the long, dark road
Where light, at each distant turn,
Falls upon unharmed leaves
To assure our gaze
That no fear lies ahead,
Nor need stay within.
There on the unleveled way
Is a steadfast hand
To hold us
To heal us
To save us
When we fall.
Let breath be still in the dim unknown.
As silent moon in drifting clouds,
The gentle streams, over guiding rocks,
Soft twilight chants of woodland birds,
The distant dance of firefly light,
The sacred hush of sleeping flowers,
The noble guard of forest trees
With nature sing to spangled skies
Reminding us
To be still
To trust
To believe
As hope whispers to our souls
In the night.
To be strong,

To love,
Perchance to dream,
As hope whispers
To our hearts
With its light.

His Amazing Love

In mystery and miracle
Love came to earth to dwell
To give us strength
And tongues of fire.
Your joy proclaim, good news to tell—
The wonders of Your love.

You call us, Lord, to follow You
In trust and faithfulness.
Let actions, Lord, speak beyond words.
Through caring hearts, let us confess
The challenge of Your love.

Give me Your love, Your saving grace.
These are Your gifts for me
To do Your will
And nothing else.
To hear Your Word that sets me free,
This is Your call of love.

The greatest gift that we can give
Is to share our love.
He knows our need.
He hears our cry.
He rescues us; give thanks to Him
For His unfailing love.

A covenant of forgiving love—
No sin where hope is told.

Wait, trust, be still,
And do God's will.
New miracles each day unfold
From His amazing love.

Great Are You Lord

Holy Lord, most holy Lord,
You alone are worthy of our praise.
Oh, holy Lord, most holy Lord,
We will sing all our days.
Great are You, Lord.
Great are You, Lord.
Great are You, Lord.
Great are You, Lord, most holy Lord.

God is faithful; He provides.
He knows our need; in Him we abide.
Sing, "Hosanna," to the King.
Salvation to us He brings.
Great are You, Lord.
Great are You, Lord.
Great are You, Lord.
Great are You, Lord, most Holy Lord.

Still today the world needs peace.
Olive branches, palm leaves,
Words of hope and love.
Hearts that praise
And lives that seek
To follow God's will above.

Praise the Lord,
Praise the Lord.
Let the people of the world

Praise the Lord.
Let God's peace reign on the earth
In salvation we find our worth,
In Christ's love our second birth. Praise the Lord!

Let Every Heart His Praises Sing
(Music: Prelude from *Te Deum* by Charpentier)

Hosanna to God, sing praises.
Hosanna to Jesus, the Lord, the King of kings.
Cry, shout, lift your voice, and praise Him!
Let ev'ry heart His praises sing.

Rejoice! Rejoice! Sing praises.
Rejoice! For the Lamb of God comes to reign on high.
Rejoice! Rejoice! Sing praises.
The world's salvation has drawn nigh.

The rising sun,
The starry skies,
The sparrow, bright flowers, and butterflies—
Nature unfolds its bright array,
God's handiwork on full display.

Oh come, let us praise the Savior.
Oh come, let us worship and bless His holy name.
For God has shown us His favor.
His truth and mercy we proclaim.

Praise God with the sound of trumpets.
Praise Him with the lute and harp; clap your hands and dance.
Let our joyous anthems praise Him.
And thank Him for His providence.

Hosanna, to God, sing praises
Hosanna to Jesus the Lord, the King of kings.
Cry, shout, lift your voice, Hosanna!
Let ev'ry heart His praises sing.

Quiet Devotion

When daylight dawns
and the birds begin to sing,
when stars seem to fade away
the morning star in my heart
new mercies bring
to guide my whole life through the day.
When I pray to You in quiet devotion,
at that moment I have all that I need.
My life is filled with the promise of Your love.
My soul finds true hope and peace.
And when I trust and believe
that You're always near
I find the courage to face my doubts
and darkest fears.
I love You, Lord; with all my heart. I love You, Lord.
I give my life to You in gratitude.
Your arms embrace all my sins
with healing grace.
My soul and my heart You renew
and ev'ry day I will sing
all my praise to You.
Till, when in joy, I see You face to face.
Amen.

Your Compassion Seeks to Find Us

Lost like sheep without a shepherd,
Your compassion, Shepherd friend,
seeks to find us
with a love our souls to mend.

Comfort from Your touch does heal us
When we know Your grace profound.
In Your arms, Lord,
Bring us home where love abounds.

Such compassion,
Shepherd friend,
Seeks to lead us through each day.
Love, so amazing, is our shelter
when, unaware, we lose our way.

Your kind hands with care embrace us
In the safety of Your fold
Where You promise
Your salvation to behold.

From the snares of death release us.
Let forgiving waters flow
Into each heart
To calm and restore our souls.

Such compassion,
Shepherd friend,
Seeks to lead us through each day.

Love, so amazing, is our shelter
when, unaware, we lose our way.

Good Shepherd friend, too long we've roamed.
Hear the fervor of our plea
To find Your peace
And dwell forever in eternal light with Thee.

The Carrying Power of Love

We sing of life
Our endless song
That turns our burdens into wings.
In prayer and quiet thought
We trust, oh Christ, Your love within us
and hope of glory to make us strong.
Oh, source of comfort and of peace
You hold us through adversity
With the carrying power of love.
When one day we breathe our last
Your everlasting arms will embrace us
Wth joy eternally.
Christ, You turn our burdens into wings,
You are our hope, the promised gospel story
In contemplative trust.
You give us strength;
We give You all the glory.
You heal the broken places of our hearts,
Turning burdens into wings!
We lift our love to You,
And filled with joy
Our hearts in thanks and praise
Will forever sing.

(Inspired by James Stewart's words: Christ in me, means Christ bearing me along from within. Christ the motive-power that carries me on. Christ giving my whole life a wonderful poise and lift, and turning every burden into wings. All this is in it when the apostle speaks of "Christ in you, the hope of glory." (Col 1:27 NRSV). Hendrickson Publishers Inc. copyright 1989 by the

Division of Christian Education of the National Council of the Churches of Christ in the USA) From *A Man In Christ*, by James S. Stewart, Regent College Publishing 1935 5800 University Blvd. Vancouver, BC Canada V6T Mr. Bill Reimer, Copyright Office.)

The Presence of Your Face

There was something in the water
That held the mystery to turn it into wine.
There was something deep within me
That yearned to make me fully Thine.
There was something in the water
That calmed the raging storm, a peace that made it still.
There was something deep in my mind
That changed my life to seek Your will.
There must be something in the water
That You share with us to drink.
There must be something in Your sacramental words
Of love that causes me to think
Of how You fill my life with joy overflowing,
With promises of grace.
There is something in the quiet streams
That I can see—
It is the presence of Your face.
There is something in the water
That can change our hearts of stone into hearts of love.
There is something in our thirsting
That draws God's Spirit from above.
There is something in the water
That washes our sins away and restores our souls.
There is something in its blessing
To heal us and to make us whole.
There must be something in the water
That You share with us to drink.
There must be something in Your sacramental words

Of love that causes me to think
Of how You fill my life with joy overflowing,
With promises of grace.
There is something in the quiet streams
That I can see—
It is the presence of Your face.

Response to Psalm 5

My grieving heart,
My sighing soul,
This crying voice,
This prayerful lamentation,
My pleading hands,
My longing eyes
All are watching,
Waiting,
Trusting, clinging
On to hope
To keep me singing.
Evil is not a companion
That walks the pathway of Your heart.
Deliver us from evil
When it tempts us
To blindly walk another way.
From falsehood lead us to light and truth.
May all hatred, our deceitful nature,
Be changed by the nature of Your grace.
Your heart swings wide the kingdom door
Where in love,
Your arms embrace us,
So we might know You.
They hold us still.
They bid us welcome to abide
In Your purpose and your will.
Where in praise and adoration,
In awe, we bow in contemplation

With our earnest supplication,
Lord, for You to show us how to live.
Sharing peace,
To be kind and just,
Not tearing down,
But building up
To heal, restore, and to forgive.
Like the night You shared with us the bread and cup.
In You, Oh God, we rejoice.
We follow You, we heed Your voice.
You bless the righteous. They know Your favor.
Teach us how to love You more and to love our neighbor.
For love can cast out every fear,
So we can ever sing for joy
In all our sorrows, in all our tears.

(Inspiring Response to Psalm 5:11–12 (NRSV) 2016 NRSV New
Revised Standard Version, Hendrickson Publishers Inc. copyright 1989 by
the Division of Christian Education of the National Council of the Churches
of Christ in the USA).

Through It All

When life's unkind,
When we are stressed,
The heart is breaking,
And there is no peace or rest.
When life's unfair
And treats us wrong,
We wonder if God
Is there at all.
Through fear and loss,
Each tear and pain,
In each dark trial
What is there to gain?
Through each doubt and shattered dream,
We wonder how to get through it all—
Through it all, when faith is weary;
Through it all, when hope is gone;
Through it all, when God is silent;
Through it all, when we feel alone;
Through it all, when our soul needs healing;
Through God's grace our sins atone.
Through it all,
Through it all,
Through it all,
He bids us follow.
The Savior calls.
Eternal life
He offers all.
Christ leads the way

Whatever befalls.

Just take His hand;

By your side He'll help you stand—

Through it all, when faith is weary;

Through it all, when hope is gone;

Through it all, when God is silent;

Through it all, when we feel alone;

Through it all, when our soul needs healing;

Through God's grace our sins atone.

Through it all,

Through it all,

Through it all,

My Savior leads me.

"All the way my Savior leads me.

What have I to ask besides,

Can I doubt His tender mercy?

Who through life has been my guide?

Heavenly peace, divinest comfort,

Here by faith, in Him to dwell.

For I know what'er befall me

Jesus doeth all things well.

For I know what'er befall me,

Jesus doeth all things well."

He has been through it all

He leads us, makes us strong

This is our song!

("All The Way My Savior Leads Me," words by Fanny J. Crosby 1820-1915 public domain)

The Silence of Forgiveness (The Prodigal)

I yearn for all I've lost
When drawn away from home.
The love I knew there
Through all these years
Still knows my name.
Love, in all its yearning
Follows each step I take
And seeks me as its child,
Waiting for a warm illumination.
When on the path that weaves uncertain,
To a nowhere destination
I discover I have no where left to go.
Turning home,
Love sees me from a far-off place.
With its familiar face
With a remembrance of its grace,
Love runs to embrace my disappointments.
Holding my failures in its surprise
Love speaks not a sound
Until I know.
I have found,
In my halted running,
That drawing me all my life was
The silence of forgiveness.

The Promise of Unfailing Love

Springs of strength,
Like peaceful waters, ebb to the place
That thirsts to know forgiveness.
A living stream
That carries every care
Like emerald leaves on a quiet prayer
When we feel like brittle paper tossed
In the wind and air.
Planted deeply by living streams
We seek the scent of unfolding grace
And find hidden in God's face
His promise of unfailing love.
Whoever truly lives,
Whoever truly loves,
Knows truly this—
The One whose finger splashed light upon the dark
Takes the chaos of our imperfection,
And touching it with His love
Calls us into life.
(Job 14:9 at the scent of water it will bud and put forth twigs like a sapling.
yet at the scent of water it will bud and put forth shoots like a plant. at the
scent of water it will bud and sprout again
Psalm 1: 3 (NRSV) New Revised Standard Version, Hendrickson Publishers
Inc. copyright 1989 by the Division of Christian Education of the National
Council of the Churches of Christ in the USA).

Come and Follow Him

Follow, come and follow Him.
Leave all that you have behind.
Follow, come and follow Him.
Find all you are meant to be.

Follow, come and follow Him.
He'll show you the way to life.
Follow, let your heart believe
His Truth that will set you free.

Follow, come and follow Him.
With a yearning heart for God
In you, let His image be,
So His love the world can see.

Follow, come and follow Him.
His Word will make all things new.
Myst'ries of the Kingdom see
In the blessed Trinity.

Follow, come and follow Him.
See the miracles He can do.
Follow, come and follow Him.
Greater things He'll do through you.

Follow, come and follow Him.
Love's kingdom work to do.
Come, His disciple be.
Let others find God through you.

Follow, come and follow Him.
There are many lost in sin.
Cast your nets into the sea,
Winning hearts for eternity.

God Is With Us

God is with us,
Embracing the world with His love.
God is with us,
Filling hearts with His light from above.

God is with us.
Let us welcome His Spirit with praise.
God is with us.
We will thank Him,
Adore Him,
Forever implore Him
To give the earth peace as we pray.

God is with us.
We are safe in His comforting wings.
Come worship Him.
Every day of our living His praise to sing.

God is with us.
There is nothing in life we should fear.
God is with us.
Through every dark trial He's near.

Rejoice; be glad.
He turns to joy each heart that is sad.
Come, celebrate.
Lift your eyes.
Face tomorrow.

Let Him hold your sorrow,
And walk in His unfailing grace.

God is with us.
We are safe in His comforting wings.
Come worship Him,
Every day of our living His praise to sing.

We thank You, Lord,
For giving us life in Your ways.
We thank You, Lord,
For giving us hope every day.

Help us be strong.
Let our love heal the earth of all wrong.
We thank You, Lord,
For Your promise and mercy.
Let all living things see
Your glory and majesty.

Something of Love

When the nights are long,
When life's pain is strong
Hold me in Your heart.
Take my hand; help me to feel
Something of stars,
Something of peace,
Something of love.

When I lose my way,
When my voice can't sing
Hold me in Your heart,
And let Your song of life bring
Something of home,
Something of joy,
Something of love.

When fear fills my mind,
When doubt makes me blind,
Hold me in Your heart
Till in my heart I can see
Something of faith,
Something of hope,
Something of love.

Yours, Lord

Yours, Lord, is the greatness and the power,
The glory, the splendor, and the majesty.
Everything in heaven and on earth is Yours, Lord.
All things come from You.
It is only of
Your gifts,
Your blessings,
Your life,
Your love
That I give to you.
I give You my life.
Through Your grace, Lord,
My deepest longings are satisfied.
Receive, oh God,
The harvest of my
Hope and
My confidence in You.
When I was born You gave me life.
Oh, Lord, at my end
I bring to You my open hands
Holding only my praise and gratitude
For all I was meant to be,
For all You were to me.
My empty hands,
My thankful heart,
My songs of praise
Are Yours, Lord.

My Love for Him

In His eyes I see,
In His voice I hear,
In His heart I find
His love for me.

Through His touch I feel,
Through His joy I know,
Through His grace receive
Love's gift of life
That sets me free.

Trusting in Him,
His blessings are mine,
Growing in the power of His Word.
That Word restores my soul.
God's Spirit makes me whole.
All praise to Him belongs.

In my eyes He'll see,
In my voice He'll hear,
In my heart He'll find
My love for Him

I will gladly show
All I am, I owe.
The whole world will know
My love for Him.
My love for Him.
Only Him.
Just for Him.

Still

Still the sun rises.
Still the birds chant.
Still the moon glows.
Still. the river flows; still
flowers that close in the friendless night
will open in the warm morning light
when all of nature
and the empty tomb
shout new life!

Still the rain falls.
Still the clouds roll.
Still the rainbow shines.
Still the morning glories climb.
Hearts that close in fear
will open as the morning appears
when all of nature
and the risen Lord
shout new life!

We will hear Him speak words of love
And call our name
to follow Him beside still waters.
We will hear Him speak words of love
if we trust His will,
if we just be still,
if we just be still
and know that
He is God!

Jesus, You Are All the World to Me

Let us praise the Lord, just praise the Lord!
Let us thank the Lord, just thank the Lord!

Let our voices shout, and praise His glorious name.
Let our voices shout, and praise His glorious name.

Let us Praise the Lord.
Let us Praise the Lord.
Let us Praise the Lord.
Let us Praise the Lord.

Lift your hands and praise.
Lift your hands and praise.
Lift your hands and praise.
Lift your hands and praise.
Lift your hands and praise.
Lift your hands and praise.
Praise the Lord!
Praise the Lord!

Jesus, You are all the world to me.
Your grace shows me all that I can be.
In Your strong arms of love
Lift me to God above.
I am Your happy child when held in Your strong embrace.
I am filled with joy when I look into Your face.

Jesus, Your hands of love carry me.
You called children to rest on Your knee.
In kingdom love to grow,
Your Word of life to know,
And through our songs Your love to show.
You will guide me;
Be always be-side me.
Your hand to lead me
When I lose my way.

Jesus, in Your eyes, Your dreams I see
Such abundant life flowing free—
Abundant life in store for me.
I give my life to You.
I'll praise You my whole life through,
And thank You for giving me Your love.

Let's just praise the Lord, just praise the Lord!
Let's just praise the Lord, just praise the Lord!

You will guide me,
Be always beside me.
Your hand to lead me
When I lose my way.

Jesus, You are all the world to me.
Your grace shows me all that I can be.
In Your strong arms of love
Lift me to God above.
Hold me close with Your Father's love.

Let's just praise the Lord, just praise the Lord!
Let's just praise the Lord, just praise the Lord!
Let's just praise the Lord, just praise the Lord!
Let's just praise the Lord, just praise the Lord!

Praise the Lord!

God's Loving Embrace

And now let grace and peace protect you;
May they give to you the joy of life complete.
May you feel comfort and contentment
As you rest and trust in God's loving embrace.
The butterflies,
The fields of lilies,
Birds of the air—
They trust in You to meet their needs.
Under God's wings, gently sustaining,
God will enfold you at the table where He feeds
The bread of life.
Our sins forgiven,
Our souls made whole,
Our faith restored,
Christ healing our strife.
And now may grace and peace embrace you
With light and life.

A Quiet, Peaceful Place

We thirst for a quiet, peaceful place
Where the joy of life is found,
A solitude in which the Holy Spirit
Breathes a sacred sound.
To lean upon the breast of Christ,
We hear a hopeful heartbeat,
and in that embrace we know that God is near.
We abide in love
And receive the gift of mercy and redeeming grace.
Our deepest prayers
At last have found, with God's presence in our soul,
A quiet, peaceful place.

Thou Art the Christ

Christ.
Thou art the Christ!
Mystery of creation,
Promise of salvation
With praise we sing.
Thou art the Christ!

Christ gives us peace,
Not as the world.
Christ gives us love
We cannot comprehend.
His peace,
His love
In Eucharistic blessing
Flows to every soul with life
That never ends.

Christ holds our hearts
In His care
And feeds our famished spirits,
Not just with food or bread
But shares
The hope
Of every Word of God.
Christ has compassion
On those who wander
Like sheep without a shepherd,
Far from His embrace.

His suffering is love's promise
Of God's redeeming grace.

And this we call to mind,
And in assurance find
God's steadfast love
Are mercies that are kind.
Great is Your faithfulness.
Teach us to faithful be
To that tree upon the rock.
Let no door, no heart, nor creed, nor church
Be a stumbling block
To prodigals who seek
Their distant home
Where they find the
Waiting Father's arms
From whom they turned and roamed.

Make us humble, serving others—
Stranger, outcast, sister, brother—
That through our loving,
Through our living,
In true compassion
And forgiving
We might live in harmony
And all the world Your kingdom see
As we proclaim,
Thou Art the Christ.
Thou Art the Christ.

Miracles Fill Each Day

A sunbeam falls.
The robin calls.
Children laugh and play.
A tree grows tall.
No dream is small.
Miracles fill each day.

A flower blooms.
The heart makes room
For love to display.
A kind, good deed
For those in need,
Miracles fill each day.

We all can share
And show we care
Through the words we say.
Flickering lights
Bring hope in sight.
Miracles fill each day.

We believe in miracles,
Not just in miracles *out there*!
Look in your heart;
Find something astounding.
We are the miracle,
And one way or another
We'll make a difference
In the world and each other.

We cry for peace.
Some starve for bread,
Need a safe, warm bed.
So let us start
Through our hearts, so
Miracles fill each day.
If tomorrow
Brings us sorrow
Give us strength, we pray.
Let us shine bright
Through the dark night.
Miracles lead the way.

Let us believe in miracles,
Not just in miracles *out there*!
Look in your heart;
Find something astounding.
We are the miracle,
And one way or another
We'll make a difference
In the world and each other.

Some see war every day.
Will we hear their sorrow
Or just turn our eyes away?
All the earth longs for peace,
For a heart that is kind.
People to heal earth's bitter strife
Till the world finds its song
And love takes wing.

For all earth's children,
For God's world let us pray.
Let us feed the hungry.
Clothe them with our love.
Let us give the world peace
By filling it,
By filling it with our
Miracles of love.

A Love of One Weaving

Beneath the cross
lies a robe of one weaving,
a remnant of God's unfailing love,
a robe of one weaving.
One thread of love flowing through our Savior's heart
Binding us in His perfect grace
In His love of one weaving,
woven through our hearts
so nothing could tear us from His love.
From our birth
to our last sigh,
God weaves His love
to bind us in
one faith,
one hope,
one baptism
in the fullness of His love,
through His love of one weaving.
Neither death, nor life
can separate us from
the love He wore,
the love He shared,
His love of seamless weaving.
Our Lord took our sins upon Himself
and wore them on the cross
in a love of one weaving.
(Text: John 19:23 "When the soldiers had crucified Jesus, they took his
clothes and divided them into four parts, one for each soldier. They also took
his tunic; now the tunic was seamless, woven in one piece from the top. So

they said to one another, "Let us not tear it, but cast lots for it to see who will get it." "This was to fulfill what the scripture says, "They divided my clothes among themselves and for my clothing they cast lots." New Revised Standard Version.) New Revised Standard Version, Hendrickson Publishers Inc. copyright 1989 by the Division of Christian Education of the National Council of the Churches of Christ in the USA).

Swaddling Love

When the Savior was born, as He slept in their wings,
The angels did sing of God's swaddling love.

Through all His life, dark trials and storms,
When our needs took His strength
Made Him tired and worn,
In deep agony and Gethsemane prayer,
God's angels held Him in their swaddling care.

Before His breath was silenced in death,
Jesus gave His Spirit into God's hands.
Then God took His Son's Spirit into His hands,
As a heart-pierced mother and heartbroken friends
Swaddled their Savior in their arms,
Walking grief's pathway
From the cross to the tomb,
Sealing His body in earth's darkest room.

The moon turned red; the sun fled the sky.
Cold stone and white shroud sealed
Hope from their eyes.
But early on Sunday, hope moved the still air,
And the good news of God's loving promise,
Mingled with their tears and their fears.
And on the third day all nature shouted its praise,
"Hope is alive! Christ is risen today!"
The cloths were folded on the stone
For Jesus had risen in splendor, our sins to atone.

Rejoice! Rejoice!
This Easter day! Jesus is risen,
Preparing the way to heaven above,
Re-clothed in glory, in God's swaddling love.

So Many Rooms

When Jesus was a boy
His mother told him of the night of joy,
When 'neath the stars of Bethlehem
He was born in a cattle shed
As angels held Him in their wings
And sang of peace 'round His manger bed.
He learned of God at Mary's knee—
Of forgiveness, love, eternity.
Through eyes of wonder He heard her say,
"There was no room in the inn that Christmas day,
So God appeared that night on starlit hay."
The holy Child, born among the lambs,
Grew to be a shepherd, whose caring hands
Gave us life, made the wounded whole,
With broken bread, restored our souls.
When cold hearts made no room for those in sin
And injustice would not let love enter in
He opened a heart of many rooms, so many rooms,
That only kingdom love could show.
When He died, was laid to rest,
He took our place within the tomb,
Where grace proclaimed we would find no room,
That we would be with God in His
many rooms, so many rooms.
Rememb'ring his troubled heart as a boy,
When told there was no room that night of joy,
Our Savior told us of many rooms, so many rooms.
He told us to not let trouble fill our breast or soul with fear,

But gave us this promise upon which we could rest,
that His Father's heart is always near
With many rooms, so many rooms,
A treasure store of love, of light,
Of peace and joy
Where we will live forevermore
In His heart of many rooms, so many rooms.

(John 14:2-4 Good News Bible, Today's English Version "In my Father's house are many rooms. If it were not so, would I have told you that I go to prepare a place for you?[a] 3 And if I go and prepare a place for you, I will come again and will take you to myself, that where I am you may be also." Second Edition 1992 American Bible Society)

One Last Tear (Lacrima Mortis)
Song of Joseph of Arimathea

Against the black sky
Fades His skin of gray.
His blood runs still.
His body slowly chills.
Joseph remembers how Christ shared
Our laughter and our tears
And spoke the words
that gave us life
and love to cast out all our fears.

"My Lord does not deserve
This vulgar end.
But see, upon His cheek
There rests one last word of love.
I heard His sigh, when He closed His eyes to die,
Then saw Him shed one last tear."

Lacrima Mortis
Lacrima Mortis
One last tear,
Promising heaven
With no more death,
No more darkness,
No more fear,
Where we would cry the last of tears.

No life moves within His breast.
His body hangs in tortured death.

Sin nails Him to the cross.
Love flows from His crown,
As we in grief and sorrow drown.
And the Lord's dear, dear friend in deep despair
Said he would sell all he owned if he
Could save him from this agony.
But there was only one last thing
That he could do for Him.
So Joseph took the body of Jesus to his garden,
A place to rest in earth,
Where they used to speak of eternal things
And share the secret of our second birth.
And Joseph said, "Oh, Lord, take this place meant for me
As You took my place upon that tree.
Let my love
Do this one last thing for You
As You cried one last tear for me.
Find rest from Your fevered soul
Rest from all Your fears
Rest, at last, from all Your tears."

Lacrima Mortis
Lacrima Mortis
One last tear,
A living stream
The promise of heaven
With no more death,
No more darkness,
No more pain,
No more fear

Where we,
One day,
Will cry the last of tears.

The Liberating Word of Love
(Tune: Jerusalem)

From God's kind heart
Compassion flows.
Love on a cross, true love we know
In mercy's liberating word.
Our lives are changed.
In faith, we grow.
Grace heals through wounds.
Hope shines through pain.
Our joy, eternal life to gain.
Forgive! Forgive!
Is the word
That frees our souls
From sin and strife.

Come, Spirit, come.
Fill us with light
Remove the dimness of our sight
When ritual and piety
Conceal the nature of Your grace.
Break down the walls that separate.
Soften all hearts where there is hate.
With tongues of flame, let us proclaim
The liberating word of love.

Praise God from whom
All blessings flow.
Through our witness may all know
The promise of redeeming love,

Justice, compassion our hearts to show.
The cross stands stripped
Of all but love.
Salvation's song
"God reigns above."
And we will share
In ministry the word of love
Till all are free.

She Bore Her Grief Standing

There stood on a hill a cruel cross of wood, where Jesus was
crucified.
In sore pain, Mary stood watching these things,
as she bore her grief standing,
as she bore her grief standing.

When He looked to the skies, groaning why He was forsaken
on that bitter cross of wood,
her soul understood. When a spear pierced His side,
the words Simeon once to her did confide
that the thorns He would wear
would turn her joy to despair
as love's agony pierced her own heart.

Beneath the dark sky she bore her grief, standing
by that shameful cross of wood,
as nails held His hands to the tree of redemption—
hands once held by her own.
The gift of salvation the world misunderstood,
God's best gift of love ever known.

The women, in anguish, cried and wailed
watching the terror of death's sting
as Mary wept for the Lamb, her son now mocked as king.
The guards tore His garments,
casting lots for His robe, at the foot of the cross unfurled,
as the scorn of the crowd on Jesus was hurled,
not knowing the blood flowing down the cross of wood

to the stone where they stood,
would atone for the sins of the world.

The Savior was placed in a garden tomb,
as Mary stood in her place grieving
for God's incarnate love born within her womb.
Watching these things, the truth was revealed,
as in the stone grave His body was sealed.
The child she bore, bore the sins of us all.
Still her soul magnified the Lord
in silence,
in sorrow,
in suffering,
in strength,
with faith in God who had done great things for her.
Then came the mem'ry of wise men, with their strange gift
of myrrh,
given to her child born king
as she bore her grief standing,
as she bore her grief standing, standing, watching these
things.

(Luke 23: 49 The Crucifixion Scene of the women standing nearby watching
these things. New Revised Standard Version, Hendrickson Publishers Inc.
copyright 1989 by the Division of Christian Education of the National
Council of the Churches of Christ in the USA).)

Next to Him (Song of the Thief)

All my life I wandered
In the darkness of my deceits
My conscience hid beneath the sinful instincts of my resistant
heart,
Giving no thought to what was wrong or right.
Trapped in
The prison of the night,
I was restless;
I had no peace.

One day as He crossed my path,
To a crowd I heard Him say
that we must turn from sin, find liberty.
He claimed He came to set the prisoner free.
He invited me to live by His side. And by my side
He would always be.

Next to Him,
I die—next to Him!
I am the one who deserves this place.
Next to Him, no other provides such grace.

When He crossed my path
I never knew one day I'd walk with Him
On the way that led to a cross.
Led to die, my just reward,
But this man hanging next to me
Has done no wrong.
For my sin He dies. He is the Lord.

He dies, yet does not speak of death.
I see paradise in His eyes,
Which speak of hope, so I might live.
Today, eternal life He gives.

He said He would remember me.
Those hands stretched out upon the tree
In paradise would reach to welcome me
To take me by the hand
So I could stand in glory next to Him.

It Was the Kiss

A streak of pain, of agony,
A path upon His cheek.
Red stains and tears that fall,
Made by our sins, the bitter
Poison and the gall,
As He carries His cross
On the path through
The city wall
To be crucified on Calvary,
To die for us all.

The raucous crowd cries, "Crucify!"
They spit, and mock, and scorn.
Mary grieves, and she mourns,
Yet knows for this He was born.

It was not the flogging that inflicted pain,
Nor the thorns that ripped His skin
Or the nails that tortured Him,
Or the piercing of His side,
Or the tearing of His clothes
That caused His deep sorrow.
It was something more painful than these—
A greater agony.
It was the agony of a kiss.
It was the agony of a betrayer's kiss
Upon the cheek
Where love flowed down.

No love
In all the world was greater than this,
Nor any agony greater than a kiss.

(Inspired by article Blog by Martyn Percy, Remorse and Redemption in Judas
and Jesus/Christ Church, Oxford University/Cathedral Blog April 8, 2020)

It Is Finished

The wind dies,
Hangs still around the lifeless trees.
There upon the blood-stained stones and
Shadows of darkened skies,
The birds are silent in their nests;
Tears choke the sad heart in my breast.
In the shadows where Jesus dies
The warmth of life grows cold in His eyes.
It is finished.
The silence is haunting to my ears.
The earth is still
While He thirsts,
While He cries.
I hunger for His voice,
But it is finished.
It is finished
He breathes His last.
All I hear is the falling of His tears,
The falling of His tears.

(John 19: 30 "It is Finished." New Revised Standard Version, Hendrickson Publishers Inc. copyright 1989 by the Division of Christian Education of the National Council of the Churches of Christ in the USA).)

If Jesus Had to Pray, What about Me?

If Jesus had to pray, what about me?
If Jesus had to pray, what about me?
He had to fall down on His knees,
Crying to His Father in His time of need.
If Jesus had to pray, what about me?
On the ground in the garden
Of dark Gethsemane
Lay Jesus, our Savior,
Beneath a barren tree.
There on His brow,
Fear turned blood red,
Running down to the shadow of a cross
Where Jesus prayed.
In the darkness of His fears,
He prayed with all His might
For God to take away His bitter cup that night.
But when weak,
A deeper love spoke through God's Son
As He prayed for God's will to be done.
If Jesus had to pray,
If Jesus had to pray,
Our prayers can make us strong like Him.
Our prayers guide us when hope is dim.
So much in life holds us to sin.
He wants so much to hold us close to Him.
If Jesus had to pray,
What about me?

If Jesus had to pray,
What about me?

(Luke 22: 42 Garden of Gethsemane NRSV New Revised Standard Version, Hendrickson Publishers Inc. copyright 1989 by the Division of Christian Education of the National Council of the Churches of Christ in the USA).)

Crowned with Thorns that We Might Live

All our sins Christ did forgive,
Felt our hunger and our thirst.
King so worthy of our praise,
Crowned with thorns that we might live.

Omnipotent on the throne
To be adored on bended knee,
Lord of life, He gave His life—
A cruel cross our sin atones.

Towel, basin, wine, and bread,
He gave His life for us instead.
Love through tender hands was given
When nails through His palms were driven.

Compassionate, lowly, meek,
The lost God saves, our souls to keep
When we stray, and make that choice,
Still is heard the Shepherd's voice.

Robed in glory next to God,
Stripped and mocked, broken body, flogged,
Alone, thirsty, breathes His last
For His robe, their lots are cast.

Empty cross and empty tomb,
Heaven's promise of many rooms.
Grace that ends all earthly strife,
Our full joy, eternal life.

Christ Is Risen, Alleluia!
(Holst, the Planets, from Jupiter)

Christ is risen! Alleluia!
Redeemer, Lord, and King,
The good news of our salvation,
Lift up your hearts and sing!
Broken bread,
His broken body,
Sacraments of grace and love
To atone our sins by dying.
Now Christ reigns with God above.
Christ is risen! Alleluia!
Redeemer, Lord, and King,
The good news of our salvation,
Lift up your hearts and sing.
No more need to fear the darkness,
No more need to dread the grave.
Just put your trust in Jesus;
His love will light the way.
Christ is risen! Alleluia!
Redeemer, Lord, and King,
The good news of our salvation,
Lift up your hearts and sing.
If you ever feel forsaken,
Lost, confused, and all alone,
the Holy Spirit in you
Will make His presence known.
Christ is risen! Alleluia!
Redeemer, Lord, and King,

The good news of our salvation,
Lift up your hearts and sing.
Where hate, misunderstanding
Fill the world with pain and strife,
The wounded hands of Jesus
fill us with hope and life.
Christ is risen! Alleluia!
Redeemer, Lord, and King,
The good news of our salvation
Lift up your hearts and sing.

(Repeat the refrain with the following words)
Praise to God and to our Savior
And to the Holy Ghost.
We join our hearts and anthems
With all the heavenly hosts.

Glory, Honor, Praise, and Adoration

Glory, honor, praise, and adoration, let
our voices shout His holy name.
Day that left the sun in darkness, now a
dawn that leaves us not the same.

Christ is risen!
All the earth awakens,
Spreading the good news of His love.

Happy fields and laughing mountains,
bursting flowers, splashing streams,
Crickets sound all nature's chorus, butterfly
wings whisper that we're free.
Birds their carols singing,
Rain their blessings bringing,
All earth's creatures sing Your praise
In harmony.

Alleluia, Christ is risen! Wounded,
broken, all His love He gave
Through the cross within the cradle;
grace was born our souls to save.

Every tear and sorrow
Finds a bright tomorrow,
All because our Savior rose
From the grave.

Risen Christ, now lift our vision, let our
acts reveal the truth we sing
So that our lives take a cross upon them,
loving, sharing, in your ministry,
People of compassion, justice, and forgiveness
Washing feet, true servants of humility.

Alleluia, Christ is risen! Crown Him, claim
Him, Lord and King of kings!
Life abundant is His promise to those
faithful in long suffering.
Love's redeeming work is done. Alleluia!
Christ is risen, is risen today.

This Is the Promise

When our breath ceases
And life comes to its quiet rest
We find a sure release
From the labors of our living.
Through the cares that come from loving
There comes the promise we are blest.
The Spirit reawakens the joy
Of heaven's eternal peace.
Love never fades.
Light forever shines
Upon our souls, resplendent, bright.
Faith reveals its hope and mystery
That after night
Comes the morn.
We are healed, restored, made whole
Filled with life, through grace, reborn.
This is the promise, the sound of soft angel wings
That carry us to God
In whose presence
We will forever sing.

Morning Begins at Midnight

Grieving can turn the deepest joy
Into our darkest fears
But morning begins at midnight
Until the dawn appears.

Grieving can still the sweetest song,
Lost in our silent tears.
But morning begins at midnight;
Bright hope is drawing near

Grieving can make the sunlight fail.
Black is the day at noon.
But morning begins at midnight;
All nature sings in tune.

Grieving can cause the heart to break,
the mind to be confused.
But morning begins at midnight
To heal us with good news.

Grieving can make us justify
Our reasons not to live.
But morning begins at midnight;
New life to us God gives.

Grieving can make us powerless
To move the stones away.
But morning begins at midnight,
Cause love is risen today.

If morning begins at midnight
And moves in acts of grace,
Our grieving can turn to dancing
When we see Christ face to face
(Amos 5:8 "And God turns deep darkness into morning." Job 35:10 "God will give you strength in the night." NRSV NRSV New Revised Standard Version, Hendrickson Publishers Inc. copyright 1989 by the Division of Christian Education of the National Council of the Churches of Christ in the USA).)

Eternity in His Eyes

In a little while, Christ told us,
We will see Him no more.
But He would not leave us comfortless
Or alone.
With us He would always be—
Around,
Within,
Beside.
He promised His grace with us would abide
Beating in our hearts,
Singing in our joys,
Feeling all our tears,
Holding all our fears.
His Spirit to lift and cheer us
'Cause He would be always near.
In a little while, Christ told us,
We will see Him no more.
But He would not leave us comfortless
Or alone.
With us He would always be.
Those who loved Him
Upon His shoulders wept
Because they would see Him no more.
Until that day
When face-to-face they would see
Eternity in His eyes
And God's great kingdom opened wide,
Where they would live with Him—

In joy forevermore.

In peace with Him reside.

And see the radiance from His face,

The splendor and glory of

Eternity in His eyes.

(John 16: 16–24 (NRSV) "In a little while you will no longer see me." New Revised Standard Version, Hendrickson Publishers Inc. copyright 1989 by the Division of Christian Education of the National Council of the Churches of Christ in the USA).)

On This Glorious Morning

On this Easter morning
Our hearts sing with praise!
Jesus Christ is risen;
He is risen from the grave!
On this glorious morning
New life sings its song!
Joyful alleluias
To our God belongs.

All our sins forgiven
By the blood He shed;
All our lives now made whole
Through the gift of broken bread.
On this glorious morning
See hope with your eyes.
On the third day, as He promised,
He did rise!

All arrayed in splendor
Crowned the Lord of life,
He shall reign forever
Our Savior, King of kings
Through His love and mercy
To all hearts He brings.
Living water in us
His eternal springs.

We are changed forever.
We are called today

To share faith and witness
To a love that has no bounds.
To the lost and wandering
We will be Christ's light.
We were once lost sinners,
But through grace were found.

Risen Christ among us,
Empty tomb behind—
May your cross remind us
If we seek You, we shall find!
On this glorious morning
Let our voices claim,
"We are given new life
Through Your precious name."

On this glorious morning
We give glory,
We give glory,
We give glory to Your eternal name!

Eternity Is Forever

Eternal love will never fade.
Eternal light will forever shine.
While moments seem to pass away
The soul, undying, in us was made.
Life is short, like twilight skies.
The sun in cycles
Moves the dawn, displaces night,
Through celestial spaces
Shines evermore, timeless, bright.
Though dreams seem lost within the dark,
Perpetual songs rise on the wings of larks.
When beating heart slows its pace
And breath upon crystal windows leaves not its trace,
Our tears and pain are merely temporal.
But faith, like love, is unending,
And truth will forsake us never
As it speaks its mystery
To remind the heart
That from obscurity comes the morn,
That in each new moment
We are blessed.
Life is reborn,
And o'er the threshold of our minds
The promise comes to rest—
That
Eternity is forever.

The Kingdom of Our God is Near

The kingdom of our God is near; repent, believe, and see.
The first word spoken by our Lord is good news to receive.

Christ spoke of love that we might love and dream and
change and learn
of grace that sees beyond our faults; its hope within us burns.

With proof our doubts He reassures. Christ shows us He's
alive
And bids us wait His promises, soon to be realized.

Disciples gathered in one room, where gusts of wind and
quake
Made their hearts glad, their tongues rejoice; God did not
them forsake.

When you receive the Spirit's power, go witness and proclaim,
"The Savior's last word sends us forth to bring the world
love's name."

Today we live to spread the Word, through our baptismal
vows.
In ministry we work and strive to build God's kingdom now.

So let us sing this joyful hymn, and with our hearts made new
Devote ourselves to breaking bread, through prayer, our lives
renew.

(Mark 1: 15 "The time is fulfilled, and the kingdom of God is at hand; repent
and believe in the gospel." Acts 1:8 "But ye shall receive power, when the

Holy Spirit is come upon you: and ye shall be my witnesses both in Jerusalem, and in all Judaea and Samaria, and unto the uttermost part of the earth." NRSV Gethsemane NRSV New Revised Standard Version, Hendrickson Publishers Inc. copyright 1989 by the Division of Christian Education of the National Council of the Churches of Christ in the USA).)

Your Open Hands

You open Your hands
to satisfy the desires
of my longing heart.
You open Your hands.
You open Your hands.
When I lose my way
You open a road,
A journey that leads to new life.
Around each bend
There appears a brand-new day
That begins at each day's end.
You open Your hands.
You open Your hands.
You open your hands,
And place Your hands in mine.
Together we walk side by side.
When I am sad, can't stop the tears.
You open my eyes
So I can marvel at sunrise colors
In the skies,
And sunset promises
Flow from Your open hands to
Touch me with Your lasting peace.
You comfort me; my tears begin to cease.
You open Your hands.
You open Your hands.
When feeling alone and silence fills my room,
You embrace me with open arms

That hold me close upon Your open heart.
Like a flower unfolding in the light
You open my mind,
You give me sight,
You give me breath.
I know You are always near
In my darkest nights.
In Your touch,
In Your words,
In Your love
There is the mercy of Your grace
Seen in Your open wounds,
Known through Your broken bread
In the blood You shed.
I take and eat.
I remember You.
My restless soul finds a quiet rest,
And I am healed,
Restored,
Renewed
As I place my life in
Your open hands,
Your open hands.

The Gifts of Christ
(His Parting Gift of Peace)

Just as Christ has loved us
In His name we are to love others too.
His parting gift of peace He gives to us.
His grace will make all things new.

Always live in His joy.
Praising God, walk in His light.
Living by faith, God's kingdom in your sight,
Loving mercy, doing right.

Gifts of life He imparts,
His full love within our hearts.
His Spirit breathes new mercies in our souls,
His blessings to help us grow

Peace is His proclaiming gift,
Love divine His arriving gift.
Life is His abiding gift.
Hope is His residing gift.
Faith is His inviting gift.
Light for our path His leading gift,
Grace to save His redeeming gift.
Healing is His touching gift.
Forgiveness is His dying gift.
Bread and wine His transforming gift,
Heaven His dwelling gift.
Eternity His surprising gift,

The crown of life His rewarding gift.
Joy is His new dawning gift.

We love you, Lord. We thank you, Lord,
For all these gifts that You impart.

("My peace I leave with you." John 14:27 (NRSV) New Revised Standard Version, Hendrickson Publishers Inc. copyright 1989 by the Division of Christian Education of the National Council of the Churches of Christ in the USA).)

We receive everything from
your hand, Lord Jesus.
Your powerful hand stretches forth and turns
Worldly wisdom into holy folly. Your gentle hand
Opens and offers the gift of inner peace.
If ever it seems that your reach is shortened,
It is only to increase our faith and trust
That we may reach out to you.
And if ever it seems that your
hand is withheld from us,
We know that it is only to conceal
the eternal blessing
You have promised—
That we may yearn for that blessing ever more
Fervently. (Soren Kierkegaard)

And with that blessing
may we ever more
fervently sing
The Melodies of Christ

Prayer

The Moment I Look into My Heart

When I look into my heart, Oh Christ,
I don't know where to start
To give You thanks
For the life You've given me,
This beautiful world to see.
Yet all around are needs, cares, and fears
that have oppressed so many songs.
Cries of hunger, tears of pain—
So many people have no voice, no shelter from the rain.
I thank You for Your hand in each moment,
Shaping my life and all I can be.
The love of two hearts that gave me life,
That held my hand, watched me grow
To stand on my own, to set me free.
Teachers and mentors who shaped my mind
And gave me a voice, the words of a song
That would call others to sing
And help them believe
In bright tomorrows,
In themselves,
In You.
For the dreams You placed in my mind,
For the blessings each day that I find,
For the people each day You call me to walk beside.

I won't wait for special times, but celebrate life each day.
Thank you, Lord, for believing in me,
For guiding my footsteps 'neath Your protective wings.
I look to You to be strong,
To make a difference with my life every day,
To speak up, be bold, when I see something wrong,
Reflecting Your kindness and caring in all I do and say,
To see a world of wonder in the stars up above
Shining through my heart with the light of Your love,
To help others find their way.
You teach me to pray; Your Word my soul feeds,
So I might become bread for others in need.
When I look in my heart, I wonder where to start.
There are so many things for which to be thankful—
More than I can number—
Like Your grace that surpasses all my sins.
But when I wrap my busy soul in slumber
At the end of the day,
I whisper a prayer with a grateful heart
That You are with me through the night,
That I will find new joys in the morning light.
Sometimes I wonder what I can do
in life to make a difference.
And then a melody in my heart begins a new tune.
You give me a song to sing,
A heart to praise,
A desire to share each day—
The Melodies of Christ.
So when I look inside my heart
There is only one place to begin as I lift my voice

And write my words and say my prayers
and proclaim Your name.
What greater joy can there be
Than to sing Your praise all day long,
So that You might hear the melodies of my grateful heart?

Amen.

About the Author

Ronald W. Cadmus was ordained a United Methodist Minister in 1975. He is a graduate of West Virginia Wesleyan College and Drew Theological Seminary. He was installed as the 48th Minister in Line of Succession at the Historic Collegiate Church of New York City, America's oldest congregation founded in 1628, under the invitation of Dr. Norman Vincent Peale, the author of *The Power of Positive Thinking* and Senior Minister of the Collegiate Church. Installed as a Reformed Church in America Minister, he served as Minister of The Fort Washington Collegiate Church of the Reformed Church in America. The Church was recognized as Church of The Year by Prison Fellowship for its outreach ministry to inmates and their families. His ministry was in the exciting area of Washington Heights where 33 different languages were spoken in the parish setting. Ron is the author of *God's Loving Embrace: The Touch That Comforts and Restores, (published by Thomas Nelson) Still, In One Peace and Fragile Ornaments, Melting Snowflakes and The Healing Light of Christmas (Published by Circle Books).* Ron Cadmus has produced choral anthems with Joseph Martin, Kevin Boesiger, Douglas Wagner, Robert S. Cohen, Brad Nix, Margaret Rizza of London, Mario Lombardo and Warner Brothers, Dan Wolgemuth and Michael Huseman. A number of his works in collaboration with Robert S. Cohen have been written for and premiered by The Philadelphia Boys Choir – Young Ambassadors of the United States, who also premiered their major 42 minute work, GENESIS, being published by C. F. Peters. Robert Cohen's masterful work, Safe Places of The Heart, a text written by Ron Cadmus, was performed at the Commemorative Celebrations of the Arizona Memorial in Pearl Harbor as a statement of the cause of freedom for which so many people have sacrificed their lives and given their service. Ron served as a Chaplain at Ground Zero following 9/11 and his prose about his experience appears on the Artist's Registry of the World Trade Center Museum. Currently being published by Hal Leonard and Shawnee Publishers are the choral works, The Gift of Dreams to Dream, The Beauty of Life, The Joy of Simple Things and The Gift of Advent Waiting for which Ron wrote the lyrics. His work, The Silence of Forgiveness (The Prodigal Son) composed by Jen Wagner was recently premiered by the Lebanon Valley University Choir.

Printed in the United States
by Baker & Taylor Publisher Services